To the joy of belief

www.BigBellyBooks.com

Big Belly Books
P.O. Box 1127
Bellaire, MI 49615

ORDERING INFORMATION:

Individual sales are available at select booksellers and retail outlets. For information on locations or to order via the Internet, contact Big Belly Books at the address above or at www.BigBellyBooks.com. Special discounts may be available on quantity purchases by corporations, associations, charities and others.

Printed in the United States of America

10   9   8   7   6   5   4   3   2   1

Library of Congress Cataloging Data on File

Schatzer, Jeffery L., 1949-
The Elves in Santa's Workshop: Together at the North Pole/Jeffery L. Schatzer
1. Christmas Story – Fiction. 2. Photography – Fiction

Dickinson Press, Grand Rapids, MI USA – September 2009
Batch number/3634000

The Elves in Santa's Workshop

Together at the North Pole

By

Jeffery L. Schatzer

with Mark Bush, Don Rutt and Ty Smith

SC

Big Belly Books
Bellaire, Michigan

www.BigBellyBooks.com

e all know that Santa is very busy – one

night a year. He drives his sleigh around the

world and squeezes down millions of chimneys. On

that special night, he delivers toys and treats to all

good girls and boys.

A few lucky people have even seen him.

While Santa works hard at Christmastime, the elves are busy all year long. How they came to live and work together at the North Pole is a story well worth telling.

ou see, elves are very special people. In many ways they are much like you and me.

They love helping and doing nice things for others.

While they are small in size, they have big, loving hearts.

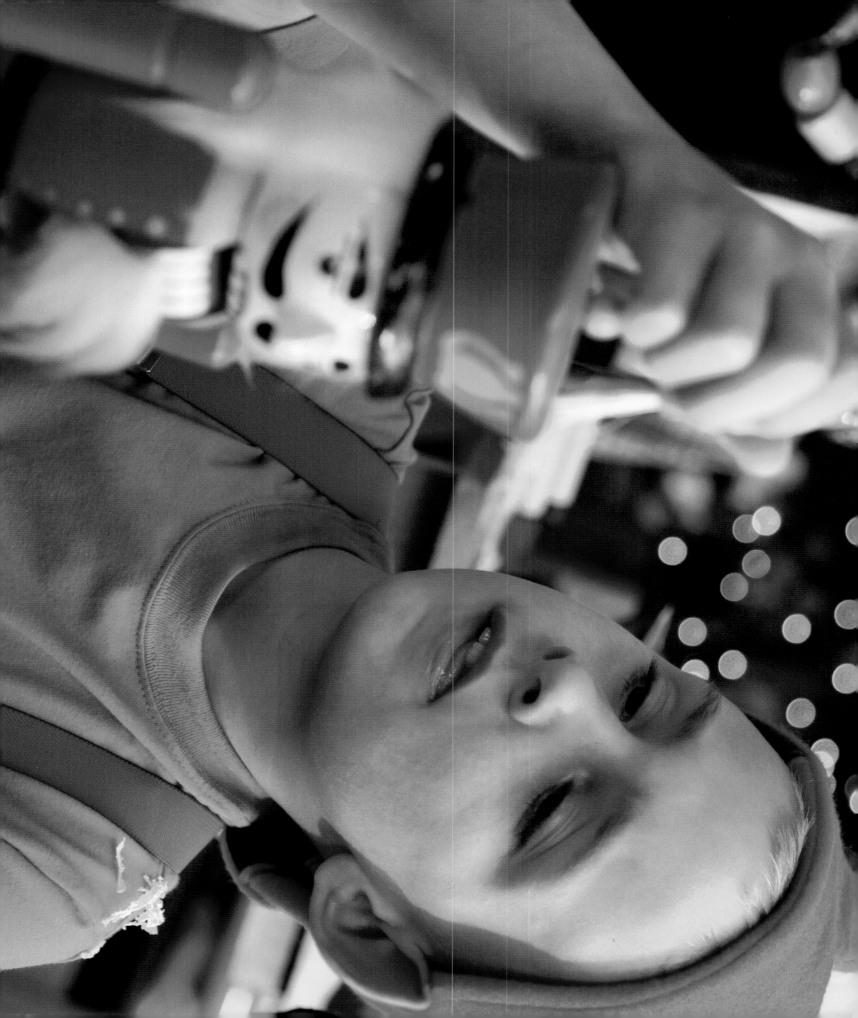

lves are creative and enjoy making things –
especially toys. They love painting and
crafts. Because elves are so thoughtful and kind,
they would rather give than receive. Elves share
nicely in all they do.

 lves have pointy ears and big, happy grins. They often wear funny clothes. Their voices are high and squeaky. They are strong and very fast. When they play, they make sure that everyone is included in their games. Elves also love school and reading, just like you.

hat you may not know about the elves is that they didn't always live at the North Pole, and didn't always work with Santa. Long ago, they actually lived among us. But, sometimes people who were bigger and stronger were not very nice to them.

The elves were pushed, picked on, poked at, and perturbed. So, they decided to move far, far away where they wouldn't be mistreated. That place was the North Pole.

The elves wrapped up all their possessions in brightly

colored paper. Then they headed north and built a

beautiful village where they could live in peace.

iving at the North Pole kept the elves safe.

But, they missed the company of others. And, they had no one to give their wonderful gifts to. The treasures they made piled higher and higher, deeper and deeper. The elves were up to their ears in gifts!

They needed help.

At the very same time Santa was having problems of his own. As more and more children came to believe in him, he just couldn't keep up with all their requests. He was up to his eyeballs in letters from good girls and boys. He needed help.

One day, a little birdie told Santa about the elves and how they had moved to the North Pole. The bird told Santa about a way to help the elves AND make sure that the children were not disappointed at Christmastime. That day Santa traveled to the North Pole.

hen he arrived, Santa introduced himself. At first the elves were afraid of him because he was so big. But, it wasn't long before Santa convinced the elves that he was kind and gentle. In a very short time they all became the best of friends.

anta told the elves about how he delivers toys to good girls and boys at Christmastime. Then he told them he needed their help to make the toys.

The elves were very happy to help. They set to work right away. Since that very day, the elves have been an important part of Christmas.

 ow you know why Santa and the elves live at the North Pole. Still, there is something else you should know. Wherever we go and whatever we do, we should always be kind to those who are smaller or somehow different. They just might be elves.

To keep Christmas alive the entire year through, give kindness in all that you share, say or do.

The Secret Writings of Santa

Deepest Appreciation

Special thanks are due to all the wonderful elves that made this book so delightful. Appreciation is extended to Shanty Creek Resorts and petsthatpull.com... Mike and Lee, Tymber, Danni Girl, Ginger Snap, Tess, Tasha Blue, and Cookie. Last, but not least, thank you to our friends at the Bay City Santa House; Mary Ida Doan; John Harley, Jr.; and the students, faculty, and staff of Old Mission Elementary School.

EMMA   Michaela   Chloe

Austin   Nicole   Hayden

    Addie   ELIZaBeth

Harrison   JaKe   JOEY